Learn Excel

A Beginners Guide To Learning Excel

By Terrence Adams

Table of Contents

Introduction

Excel is one of the best computer programs you can use to be productive. With it, you can organize activities and monitor progress. And if things aren't turning out as you thought, it can help you make appropriate decisions for the future.

The biggest problem, however, is getting started. Many seem to hit a block after entering a few numbers into the program. As a result, they give up without giving Excel a chance to shine.

But the fact is that once you get a glimpse of what the program can do, you get hooked to it. It becomes impossible to resist fitting it in almost every part of your life.

In this book, you will learn how to use Excel. Knowing that you may not have prior knowledge of the program, I tried to make all the tutorials in the book easy to understand.

But don't let that fool you into thinking that this book is for kindergarten kids; it's packed with excellent tutorials that will make you feel like you have been using Excel for years.

By the time you will get to the end, you will have discovered a couple of things Excel can help you with. So without further ado, let's get started.

I hope you will enjoy the reading.

Chapter 1: Excel 101

Microsoft Excel is a software program used for storing, organizing, and manipulating data. It is part of the Microsoft Office Suite and it's the second most used program in the Suite after Outlook.

In Excel, a saved file is called a Workbook. A page in the workbook is referred to as a Worksheet.

Why Use Excel?

The popularity of Excel is not coincidental; the software simplifies the task of working with data. And this is especially true when the amount of data is extensive.

In Excel, you can instantly filter your data to only focus on what's important. If you would like to see how your data relates to each other, the software can make graphical representations of it by putting it in charts.

One of Excel's greatest features is its ability to do math computations. Not only does this save time, but it also reduces the possibility of errors

What Can You Do in Excel

What you decide to do in Excel depends on what you want to achieve in the end. If you run a small business, your needs will surely vary from a home user. The good thing is that Excel has enough features to cover diverse needs.

Here are some things you can do in the program:

Make budgets – there are a lot of dedicated computer programs you can use when budgeting. But for most people, Excel is adequate. Even better, there are Excel budget templates you can use. Once you have one of these, your task is reduced to filling data in the appropriate cells.

Plan for activities – if you have a to-do list, Excel is a great program to use in planning those activities. Beside each activity, you can show when it must be done, its priority, etc. If short on time, this will help you focus on the most important activities.

Make invoices – if you run a freelance business, you can use Excel to track who you've worked for, how much you earned on each job, and more.

Monitor your fitness routine – working out to lose weight or stay fit becomes hopeless when you can't see where you are coming from. But this can easily be done with Excel. You can make a workbook showing the exercises you do, the amount of time you exercise daily, and how much weight you are losing. Additionally, you can easily see your improvement in fitness over time.

Make a customer database – although Excel doesn't come close to how powerful and robust Microsoft Access is, you can still make great databases in the former.

Chapter 2: Learn the Interface

Your ability to use Excel largely depends on how much you know about the program. So before we get to the "How-Tos," it important that we take time exploring the interface. You don't want to waste time trying to figure out where things are.

Ribbon

Every Excel function resides in this space. To avoid confusion, Microsoft grouped these functions into tabs. If you want to insert a chart, for example, common sense will guide you to the Insert tab.

The ribbon is dynamic: its look changes depending on the available space. On large screens, all functions are visible and they have space between them. But it's the opposite on smaller screens.

Figure 2.1

Here are the tabs found in the ribbon:

File - this is also known as the "back-stage view." Clicking this tab brings options to save your workbook, create new ones, open those you saved earlier, and other functions.

Home - this is where you'll find the most basic functions in excel. In fact, you will be spending most of your time in this tab.

Insert - if you want images, tables, charts, etc., this is the tab to activate.

Page Layout - most of the commands in this tab are to do with printing.

Formulas - when it's time for calculations, this tab will render your shiny digital calculator useless.

Review - spellings, grammar, and other options to correct mistakes are found in here.

View - this adjusts the appearance of the worksheet.

Cells

These are the small boxes that make up a worksheet. Every cell has an address, same like every house in every neighborhood. In the figure below, I have data in cell B3.

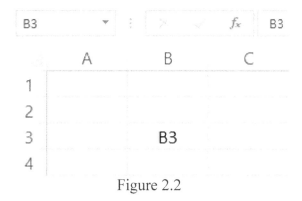

Figure 2.2

The columns are identified by letters while rows have numbers. The cell address always starts with the column letter followed by the row number.

Column Bar

The column bar has a total of 16,384 columns. These are identified by the letters of the alphabet. After Z, you start getting column names with a combination of the letters; for example, AA, AB, AC, etc.

Row Bar

This is the numbered vertical bar to the left of the worksheet. It has a total of 1,048,576 rows. Of course, you aren't going to need this many rows. And you can easily hide the ones you won't use.

Title Bar

This shows the name of the program you are using. It also has the name of the

workbook you are working on.

Figure 2.4

Sheet Area

Your data goes into this area. As you can see from the figure below, it is made up of lots of cells.

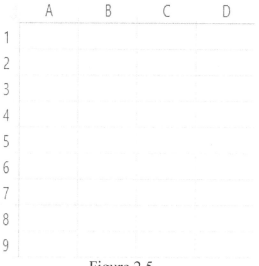
Figure 2.5

Status Bar

Like the name suggests, this bar shows more information about the workbook. Additionally, it's where zooming controls are located.

Chapter 3: The Basics

Excel has a lot of advanced features you need to know if you want to unlock its full potential. But as with every class, a great foundation is always the wisest way to get started with a lesson.

In this chapter, we will look at the basics of using Excel. These include saving, entering data, hiding worksheets, and more. If you have been using computers for a while, you may already be familiar with some of these things.

Moving Around

You have two ways of moving around in Excel: with your mouse or keyboard. The decision on which of the two to choose depends on what's most comfortable for you.

When using the mouse, you need to move the mouse pointer into a cell you want and left-click. This will activate the cell.

To highlight a cell range, you first move the mouse pointer into a starting cell. You then hold down the left button on the mouse and move until the desired range has been highlighted. In the figure below, the highlighted range is A1:B10.

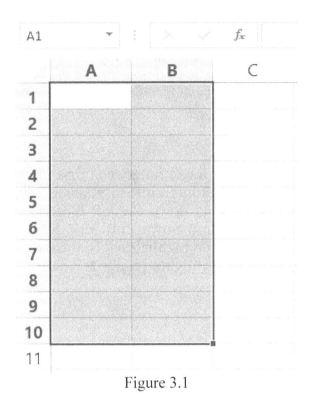

Figure 3.1

Alternately, you can achieve the same
with your keyboard. To move to a certain cell, use the arrow keys. To highlight a range of cells, get into a starting
cell, hold down the Shift key and use the
arrow keys until you get to the last cell of
the range.

Entering Data

Data is the lifeblood in every worksheet. And thankfully, entering it in the sheet is easy.

We will use the data below as an example.

Month	Number of Visitors	Income
January	50,000	300
February	55,000	322
March	61,200	400
April	62,000	450
May	63,000	470
June	57,000	390

This assumes we have a blog.

The steps below explain how you can enter this data in Excel:

1. Activate cell A1 and type the word **Month.**

2. Navigate to cell B1 and enter **Number of Visitors.**

3. Go to cell C1 and type **Income.**

4. Go to cell A2, type **January**, and press Enter. You will automatically get into cell A3.

5. Type **February** and hit enter. Fill the other cells the same way. You should finish with June in cell A7.

6. Activate cell B2 and type **50,000**. Enter the remaining values in the subsequent cells in the same way.

When done, your worksheet should look like the one below.

Figure 3.2

	A	B	C	D
1	Month	Number o	Income	
2	January	50000	300	
3	February	55000	322	
4	March	61200	400	
5	April	62000	450	
6	May	63000	470	
7	June	57000	390	
8				

A1 — fx Month

Modifying Cell Content

Assuming I made a mistake typing data in the worksheet, I can make a correction easily. For instance, let's say cell C2 was supposed to have 280 and not 300.

To correct this, activate cell C2 and enter 280. You will notice that the 300 will be erased automatically (it's unnecessary to press the Delete or Backspace key first).

Using Auto Fill

Time is everything and Microsoft understands this really well. The company has included lots of features in Excel to save time and effort. One such feature is Auto Fill.

With this, Excel automatically enters sequential data into other empty cells. This data can be numbers, days of the week, years, or even months.

Here is how to use Auto Fill when typing months:

1. Activate cell A3 with your keyboard.

2. Hold down the Shift key and press the down key until you get in cell A7. A3:A7 should be highlighted (note that you can also achieve this with a mouse).

3. Hit the Delete key to get rid of **February** to **June**.

4. Activate cell A2. Go to the little square in the right bottom corner of the cell. This is known as the Fill Handle. Your mouse will turn into a small, black cross when you get to this.

5. Hold your mouse's left button and move until you get to cell A7. This should bring back February to June.

You can also do this with numbers. Below are the steps to follow:

1. Create a new worksheet by left-clicking the + sign next to Sheet 1 at the bottom.

2. Activate cell A1 and type **2015**. Press the Enter key.

3. Type **2016** in cell A2 and hit Enter again.

4. Highlight A1:A2.

5. Move the mouse pointer to the Fill Handle and hold down your mouse's left button.

6. Move the mouse pointer until it is in cell A7.

Saving a Workbook

The whole point of entering data in Excel is to get back to it, change it, share it, and use it for decision making. The only way to ensure this is to save it.

 The steps below detail how you can save your work in Excel:

1. Click the File tab and select Save As

2. From the options, select Computer then Browse.

3. A dialog will open up. Choose Documents.

4. Write the word **Blog** in the File Name field and hit the Save button at the bottom.

When you make changes to the file, you do not need to go for the Save As option again; doing that will create a new file. Instead, you must use the Save option. This is found just above Save As. Alternatively, you can use the save option found in the Tittle bar. It has a Floppy icon and it's found next to Undo.

Hiding a Worksheet

When you have a lot of worksheets in a workbook, you will notice that some of these will get in your way. The best solution is to hide those you don't need. Use the following steps to do that:

1. Right-click the name of the sheet you want to hide.

2. Select Hide from the options.

To unhide, right-click any sheet name and choose Unhide. You should then select the sheet you want and click OK.

Deleting a Worksheet

With time, you may realize that some worksheets in your workbook are unnecessary. So these will need to be deleted.

This process is similar to hiding a work-sheet as you will witness in the steps below:

1. Right-click the name of the sheet you want to delete.

2. From the options, select Delete.

3. If you have made changes to the sheet, confirm that you want to delete by clicking the Delete button from the dialog that appears.

You may also rename a sheet in the same way. Just that instead of going for Delete, you select Rename.

Chapter 4: Editing

Even the most advanced Excel users make mistakes. But they have a secret that saves them from the embarrassment–editing. Excel has lots of editing options to give even the most shoddily done first draft a professional finish.

Find and Replace

You may want to modify some data in your workbook. If dealing with a long worksheet, this means minutes of digging to find what you want. And it's easy to miss some of this data when working like this.

Thankfully, you are now in Excel, and you can let the software do this eye-straining work on your behalf with its Find & Replace function.

Find highlights all the data you are looking for. And Replace substitutes it with the new one. The changes affect all the cells that have the value you are targeting.

To Replace a value, like Income, here is what you do:

1. In the Home tab, click Find & Select.

2. Choose Replace.

3. In the Find What space, write **Income** and click Find All

4. Go to the second space, Replace With, and write **Revenue**. You should then press Replace All.

Figure 4.1

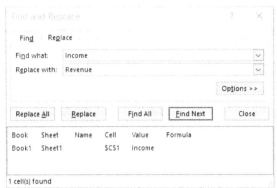

If you just want to find a value without replacing it, choose Find when you click Find & Replace.

Insert Columns and Rows

After entering data in your worksheet, you may realize that you need more rows or columns. You don't need to move data to accommodate your changes; you can simply insert new columns or rows.

Inserting a Column – we will insert it between Column B and C:

1. Activate column C by left-clicking the letter C in the column bar.

2. Click Insert in the Cells group found in the Home tab.

Inserting a row – we will have it between row 1 and row 2:

1. Activate row 2 by left-clicking 2 in the row bar.

2. In the Cells group, click Insert.

Resizing Columns and Rows

You probably have noticed that some of the content in cell B1 is not visible. This is because the column width is too small to accommodate all the words. As a solution, we must increase the column width.

There are two ways on how you can do this. Here is the first one:

1. Activate cell B1.

2. In the Home tab, click the arrow next to the Format button in the Cells group.

3. From the options, select Column Width.

4. Type **18** in the dialog box and hit OK.

Here is the second method:

1. Move the mouse pointer between the letters B and C in the column bar. Your mouse will change to a black cross.

2. Hold down left-click and drag to the left or right.

You must follow the same process when resizing rows.

For example, if trying to resize row 2, select any cell in the row. Click the arrow next to the Format button and select Row Height. In the box that appears, type in the number you want and click OK.

Conversely, you can move the mouse pointer between 2 and 3 in the row bar, press left-click, and then drag up or down.

Cut, Copy, and Paste

These are functions you can't afford to not know. They are useful for moving data and duplicating it as many times as you want.

Moving data

Again, there are two ways on how you can do this.

Here is method 1:

1. Highlight A1:C7

2. Move the mouse to the top left corner of cell A1. The mouse should change to a thin black cross with arrows on all sides.

3. Hold down left-click and move the mouse pointer to cell E2. The data should now be in E2:G8.

Here is method 2:

1. Highlight E2:G8.

2. Move the mouse into any of the high-lighted cell and right-click.

3. From the options, choose Cut.

4. Move the mouse to A1 and activate the cell.

5. Right-click and select the Paste icon.

Copying

This duplicates your data, eliminating the need to enter it again.

Let's copy the contents of C1:C7 into E1:E7.

1. Highlight C1:C7.

2. With the mouse in one of the high-lighted cells, right-click and select Copy.

3. Activate cell E1, press right-click, and choose Paste.

4. Place the Esc key on your keyboard.

Note that you can also find the Copy, Cut, and Paste functions on the left of

the Home tab.

Figure 4.2

Undo

In case you have made a change and you regret your decision, Undo is the tool to use. You can find it in the Title bar and it has an arrow

pointing to the left.

Figure 4.3

Next to it, on the right, is Redo. This brings back the changes you lost when you pressed Undo.

Let's see Undo in action:

1. Highlight C1:C7

2. With the mouse pointer in one of the highlighted cells, right-click and select Clear Contents.

3. To bring back what we just deleted, click the Undo button.

Chapter 5: Formatting

By default, Excel opens a worksheet with nothing by empty cells. It's your duty to fill these cells with data. But then, when done, the worksheet may not look the way you imagined.

This necessitates the use of formatting options to get exactly what you want. The best part is that Excel has just about every formatting feature you can ask for. And if you make a change you don't like, you can simply hit Undo.

Merging Cells

It's common to have a value that acts as an umbrella for a couple of columns or rows. And the best way to show such a value is to put in merged cells.

From our example, let's suppose the name of our blog is OurBlog.com. And we want this to span across A1, B1, and C1.

Follow the steps below:

1. Insert a new row above row 1

2. Highlight A1:C1.

3. In the Home tab, click the arrow beside Merge & Center (found in the Alignment group).

4. Select Merge & Center from the options.

5. Type the words **OurBlog.com** in cell A1.

Figure 5.1

To Unmerge, select the merged cell, click the arrow next to Merge & Center, then choose Unmerge Cells.

	A	B	C	D
1		OurBlog.com		
2	Month	Number of Visitors	Revenue	
3	January	50000	280	
4	February	55000	322	
5	March	61200	400	
6	April	62000	450	
7	May	63000	470	
8	June	57000	390	
9				

A1   fx   OurBlog.com

Changing Font Type

Since tastes differ, you may want to use a font type different from the default one. Needless to say, using another font is a great way of drawing people's attention.

Moving on with our blog example, let's change the look of OurBlog.com in cell A1:

1. Activate cell A1.

2. In the Font group, click the arrow in the font type box and choose the font you want.

3. Click the arrow in the font size box and choose 14.

Figure 5.2

On Font Color

Nothing gets attention better than a change of color. So use font color to your advantage whenever you can:

1. Activate cell A1.

2. In the Font group, click the arrow in the font color box and select what you like most (I have chosen blue).

Using Fill Color

All the cells in our worksheet have a white background. If you don't like this, you can change it to any color you want. Here are the steps to follow:

1. Select cell A1.

2. Click the arrow in the fill color box.

3. Choose a color that will blend with the font color you already chose. I've gone for gray.

Borders

You can add borders to your cells to help distinguish where things begin and end.

Let's add a border at the bottom of cell A1:

1. Select cell A1.

2. Click the arrow in the border box. The border box is to the left of the fill color box.

3. From the options, select Thick Bottom Border.

Alignment

You may have noticed that some of the data in our worksheet is pushed to the right, some is in the center, and some on the left.

Let's have everything pushed to the Left:

1. Highlight range A1:C8.

2. In the Alignment group, click Left.

Figure 5.3

If you want values on the right or center, you must follow the same steps. Just that you will select right or center.

Conditional Formatting

Another important feature in Excel is Conditional Formatting. With this, only values that fit a certain criterion are formatted, helping you focus on what's most important.

For this example, let's use Conditional Formatting to highlight all the months we received over 60,000 visits:

1. Highlight column B by clicking the letter B in the column bar.

2. In the Styles group, click Conditional Formatting.

3. Move the mouse pointer to Highlight Cells Rules, then select Greater Than.

4. In the dialog box, type **60,000** and hit OK.

Figure 5.4

To clear this, activate column B, click Conditional Formatting, move the mouse pointer to Clear Rules and select Clear Rules From Selected Cells.

As another example, let's use Conditional Formatting to see how our monthly incomes relate to one another:

1. Highlight column C.

2. Click Conditional Formatting then move the mouse pointer to Icon Sets.

3. Go through the different sets and choose the one you like most. I chose 5 Ratings.

Chapter 6: Working with Formulas

Like said earlier, one of Excel's strengths is how it simplifies calculations. When new to this, it always seems intimidating. But after you perform a couple of calculations, you'll testify that Excel is one of the best computer programs you have ever used.

Calculations You Can Do

Although Excel's calculations are done differently than when using a regular calculator, the process is basically the same. Furthermore, the result you get is also similar.

The biggest advantage of using Excel is that you save a lot of time. Furthermore,

the chance of making errors is signifi-
cantly reduced.

Here are some of the calculations you
can do in Excel:

+ for addition

- for subtraction

* for multiplication

/ for division

^ for exponent

Typing 2*2 in a cell will return 4.

You can also use cell addresses to calculate the value of the specified cells. For example, you can multiply D1 and D2. This will show the result in a cell of your choice.

But before you do any computations in Excel, you need to let the software know that it must perform a calculation. To communicate this, every calculation must begin with an = sign

Going back to our blog example, let's calculate the sum of money we received from January to June. The result must be displayed in cell C9. Here is how to proceed:

1. Activate cell C9.

2. Starting by typing =.

3. Using the mouse, select cell C3 then type +. Select cell C4 and type +. Do this

until you get to cell C8, after which you should press the Enter key. You should have 2312 in cell C9.

Figure 6.1

If we wanted to multiply the contents of C3:C8, we would have substituted + by *.

Copying Formulas

In case we also want to add B3:B8 and have the result in B9, there is no need to go through the addition process like we did above; we already have a formula in cell C9 that we can copy into cell B9. Contrary to what you would think, this will give the total of B3:B9, not C3:C9.

The following steps detail how you can copy a formula:

1. Activate C9.

2. Move your mouse pointer to the fill handle in the bottom right corner of the cell. It will change into a small + sign.

3. Drag the mouse pointer into cell B9. The answer should come up automatically.

Note that these formulas can also be used horizontally, i.e., B3+C3 and have the answer in D3.

Using Functions

Formulas are great for doing calculations in Excel. Unfortunately, they are limited in terms of what they can achieve. A solution is to use Functions. Not only are these capable of handling complex calculations, but they are also very efficient.

Going back to our example, let's recalculate the SUM of C3:C8 using a function:

1. Activate cell C9, press right-click and select Clear Contents.

2. Type **=SUM(C3:C8)** and press the Enter key. This should give the same answer as we had earlier.

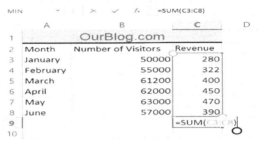

Figure 6.2

Let's calculate the average number of visitors we get each month. We must have the result in cell B9.

1. Activate cell B9 and clear its content.

2. Type **=AVERAGE(B3:B8)** and press the Enter key on your keyboard.

You don't need to memorize all the functions in Excel. There is an easy way of accessing them without memorizing a thing – the Formulas tab.

Suppose we want to determine the largest value in range C3:C8. We will need to use the MAX function:

1. Clear the contents of cell C9.

2. Select the Formulas tab in the ribbon.

3. Click More Functions in the Function Library group.

4. Move the mouse pointer to Statistical and click MAX. This will bring a dialog box with C3:C8 already selected. Since this is what we want, we just need to click OK.

Figure 6.3

Chapter 7: Using Macros

Excel has a lot of features. It's no wonder then that only a small percentage of these see the light of day. One underused feature is a macro. However, this is one thing you can't afford to not know in Excel.

A macro is a code you use to automate routine tasks. For example, if you bold, underline, and fill the background of each cell with the color green, you can make a macro of these tasks. Every time you want to execute them, you just run the macro and Excel will handle the rest.

Apart from saving you time, the other advantage is the guarantee that every worksheet will look the same (there is no chance of skipping a task when using a macro).

However, the fact that I mentioned "code" shouldn't scare you. You won't need even a single VBA coding lesson to use a macro.

Excel has a feature which lets you perform the routine tasks while it records. When done, it will translate your actions into a code.

But before you jump into the macro world, you need to know an important piece of advice: macros are very powerful. While this is a good thing, it can also be a source of concern.

If running a macro from a malicious source, you can easily lose your files in the same way you would with a computer virus. So only run macros from reputable sources.

How to Make a Macro

Let's have a macro that bolds values, increases the font size, and then changes the font color. But before we get to that,

	A	B	C	D	E	F	G
1	Item	Color	Buyer	Quantity	Unit Price	Total	
2	tablet	blue	Andy	2	99	198	
3	tablet	green	Ben	1	90	90	
4	tablet	green	Cathy	1	90	90	
5	tablet	blue	Dennis	4	99	396	
6	tablet	white	Eve	3	110	330	
7	tablet	white	Fred	2	110	220	
8	tablet	green	George	4	90	360	
9	tablet	blue	Harold	6	99	594	
10	tablet	white	Ivan	2	110	220	
11	tablet	white	Jane	1	110	110	
12	tablet	blue	Ken	3	99	297	
13							
14							

make a new worksheet that looks like the one below:

Figure 7.1

This assumes that we have an online store where we sell tablet computers.

Now that we have our worksheet, we need to record our macro. Know that once you start recording, every move you make with the mouse or keyboard goes into a VBA code.

Here is how to make a macro:

1. Click the View tab in the ribbon.

2. Click the arrow below Macros and choose Record Macro.

3. Rename the macro to **Formatting** and press Ok.

4. Go to the Home tab. Click bold, increase the font size to 12, and select the font color you want.

5. Since we have done everything we wanted, we must stop recording. To do this, go to View, click the arrow on Macros and choose Stop Recording. You can also do this by clicking the white square next to Ready in the status bar.

To run the macro, select the range you want to apply the formatting attributes to. Using the online store worksheet, let's highlight A1:F1. Go to View and click Macros. In the dialog box that shows up, select the macro you just recorded and click Run.

If you did everything right, your changes should be applied in A1:F1.

Chapter 8: Other Operations

Having come this far, I would say you are almost ready to justify paying Microsoft a couple of bucks every month so you can use Excel. However, there are still other advanced operations you must learn. Knowing these, like they say, will ensure that you get your money's worth.

Data Filtering

With this option, you can hide cells you don't want to see at that time. This is handy when you have a long worksheet.

For this chapter, we will use the worksheet of our imaginary online store.

You probably have already noticed that we offer our tablet computers in 3 colors: blue, green, and white.

Let's use the filter function so that we are only seeing white tablets sold in January:

1. Highlight column B.

2. In the Home tab, go to the Editing group and click Sort & Filter.

3. From the options, select Filter. You should now see an arrow in cell B1.

4. Click this arrow, uncheck Select All, then checkmark white and click OK.

	A	B	C	D	E	F	G
1	Item	Color	Buyer	Quantity	Unit Price	Total	
				2	99	198	
				1	90	90	
			y	1	90	90	
			nis	4	99	396	
				3	110	330	
				2	110	220	
			ge	4	90	360	
			ıld	6	99	594	
				2	110	220	
				1	110	110	
				3	99	297	

Sort A to Z
Sort Z to A
Sort by Color
Clear Filter...
Filter by...
Text Filters
Search
(Select All)
blue
green
white
(Blanks)
OK   Cancel

Figure 8.1

You should now have only 4 rows; the ones with the color white.

If you want, you can use multiple filters in one worksheet. For example, let's filter white tablets that were purchased by Ivan. This means we will have to apply filters in columns B and C.

1. Click Sort & Filter and select Filter. Doing this will clear the filter we applied earlier in column B.

2. Highlight A1:F12.

3. Click Sort & Filter and select Filter. This should bring arrows in A1:F1.

4. Click the arrow in cell B1 and only checkmark white.

5. Click the arrow in cell C1 and only checkmark Ivan.

When finished, you should only have Row 10.

Data Validation

We must acknowledge that we won't be the only ones who will be using our online store's worksheet. If we have others helping us run the business, then it's clear the worksheet will have multiple users.

To ensure that data entered in every cell is in line with what we want, we must use data validation.

If a user inputs a wrong value, Excel will give an error message. And depending on how we set it up, it will advise the user steps to take to correct the mistake.

Example

Since we only sell 3 types of tablets costing $90, $99, and $110, it means that these are the only 3 numbers that can go into any cell in column E. And we must make this clear by using data validation:

1. Highlight E2:E13.

2. Go to the Data tab and click Data Validation.

3. A dialog box will open. Click Allow and select Whole Number.

4. In the Data space, select between.

5. Type **90** as the minimum and **110** as the maximum.

6. Click the Error Alert tab (still in the dialog box).

7. Type **Wrong Value** as the title and **must be between 90 and 110** as the error message.

8. Hit OK.

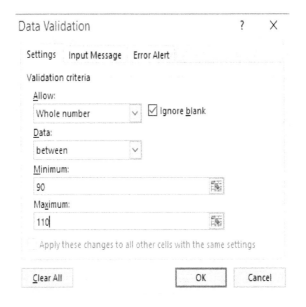

Figure 8.2

Now try entering a value outside 90 and 110 in cell E13.

We can also do the same in column B. And since we only have 3 colors, we can give the user a list to choose from. Here is how to do it:

1. Highlight B2:B13.

2. Click Data Validation.

3. In the Settings tab, select List on Allow.

4. On Source, type **blue,green,white** and hit Ok

Figure 8.3

If you select cell B13, you will see there is an arrow next to it. Clicking this will reveal the only colors you can have in this cell. If you write something not on the list, like red, Excel will not allow it.

To clear these validations, highlight the affected cells, click Data Validation and choose Any Value in the Allow box.

Alternatively, click Data Validation. When the dialog box comes up, click the Clear All button at the bottom.

Inserting Charts

Having data scattered all over the sheet area can make interpretation difficult. But you can easily get around this with charts.

The best part is that you have options as to what type of a chart to use. Also, you can format it to look in any way you want.

Let's make a chart showing the number of tablet computers each buyer bought in the month of January:

1. Highlight C1:D12.

2. Go to the Insert tab

3. In the Charts group, click Insert Column Chart and select the chart type you want.

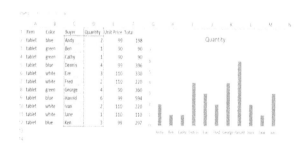

Figure 8.4

When you click the inserted chart, you will see new tabs in the ribbon called Design and Format. You can use these to transform your chart's appearance; for example, you can change color, select another chart style, add titles on the axes, and more.

I would recommend you spend some time tweaking your chart. This will help you get acquainted with using charts. And if you don't like the changes, you have a savior in the name of Undo.

One thing many struggle with is figuring out how to delete the chart they just inserted. But as you will see in the steps below, it's very easy:

1. Move the mouse pointer to the edge of the chart and left click (left-clicking the middle does not work).

2. Press the Delete or Backspace key on your keyboard.

Chapter 9: Common Shortcuts You Need to Know

Switching your hands from the keyboard to the mouse constantly can hurt your speed. The best way to avoid this is to know keyboard shortcuts that achieve the same result as using the mouse.

In this chapter, I will give you some keyboard shortcut every Excel user needs to know.

Ctrl + N	Used to create new workbooks.
Ctrl + O	Brings a dialog box you can use to open workbooks you saved earlier.

Ctrl + S	Instead of hitting the floppy icon in the title bar, use this shortcut to save a file when you make changes to it.
Ctrl + W	This closes the workbook you are currently working on.
Ctrl + C	Instead of right-clicking and choosing Copy, you can just press this keyboard combination.
Ctrl + X	This is the shortcut for Cut.
Ctrl + V	This is the shortcut for Paste.
Ctrl + Z	Keyboard combination for Undo.
Ctrl + Y	Shortcut for Redo.
F2	Edits the current cell.

Ctrl + A	This highlights all cells in your worksheet.
Ctrl + Space	This highlights all cells in the current column.
Shift + Space	This highlights all cells in the row you are working in.
Ctrl + 1	Brings up a dialog box you can use to format cells.
Ctrl + T	Creates a table from the selected data.
Ctrl + G	This is a Go To option. It helps you jump to a specific area in a long worksheet.
Ctrl + F	Brings up a dialog box you can use to Find and Replace values.

Ctrl + Home	Takes you to cell A1.
Ctrl + End	Takes you to the last used cell in your worksheet. If you have used A1:E15, this keyboard shortcut will take you to cell E15.

Conclusion

Having come this far, I would like to congratulate you for reading this book. And I'm sure it has helped you discover how to get the best from Excel.

Now that you have finished the reading, your task doesn't end here; you must keep on using Excel. That's the best way to master it. Furthermore, you must keep on learning everything you can about it.

As you have seen, the software is not difficult to use. You just need to know where to click. Once you do that, you will tremendously improve your productivity, save time, and possibly, money.